"All cities are mad, but the madness is gallant. All cities are beautiful, but the beauty is grim."

Christopher Morley

ACKNOWLEDGMENTS

I would like to thank the following people for their help in the production of this book:
Barbara Angell, Millie Mom Arthrell, Karen Bourne, Pamela Craig, Robert Drake, Michael Drexler, Joel Garson, Bob Jackson, Abraham Klein, Daniel Thompson, Barry Zuckor; and thanks to the people of Cleveland, Ohio, for providing the inspiration.

THIRD PRINTING ♦ BICENENNIAL EDITION

Cleveland State University Poetry Center

HEART'S CARGO was originally published in 1985. This 1996 reprint is sponsored as a bicentennial project by the CSU Poetry Center.

All poems are published with the permission of the authors. Special thanks to Lauren Angell for permission to reprint illustrations by the late Barbara Angell.

ISBN 1-880834-30-8

preface

Why?
Because I love this goddamn city. That's why.

Bill Arthrell, editor

for

Clare C. Haulk - a great Clevelander and
a greater uncle.

Tony and Mary Walsh - great attorneys and
greater Clevelanders.

Daniel Thompson - the main man of Cleveland
poetry.

and to the students of Cleveland Public Schools.
Thanks for teaching me.

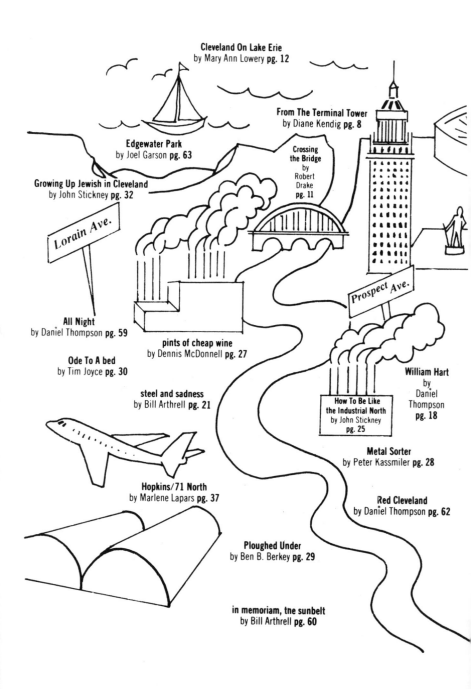

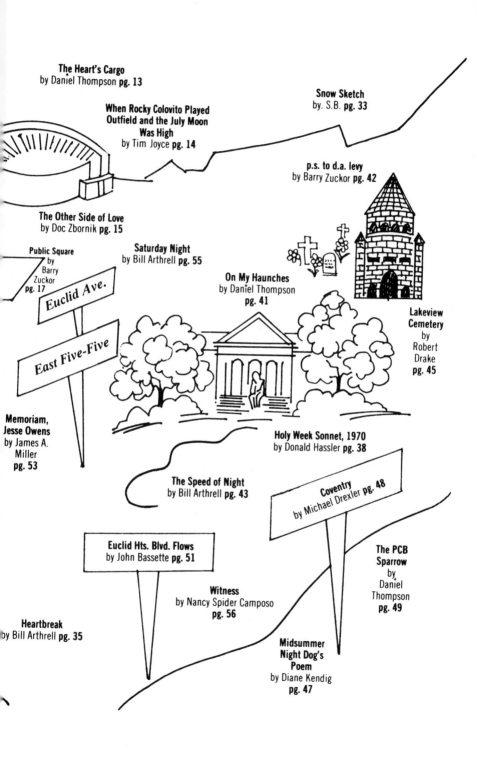

List of Illustrations

From the Terminal Tower

Lately places overlap in my memory
like the stripes in a mackerel sky,
the time between them, air, miles deep,
as invisible as never having existed.

I am standing in all the lookouts I have ever known:
my father lifts me up to this window in Cleveland
and a love points out Seville from the top of the Giralda
and alone above Niagara Falls I watch whirlpools form.

And the whole while, I am with my friends
who lingered in a fortress to watch sunset
and found themselves locked in the turret.

I'm at the end of a tangent, with snow falling
and all the color gone from a view where once even
the cars were as primary red and blue and green as toys.
And all the neon pink clouds are blinking off, stacking up gray.

Diane Kendig

Crossing the Bridge

over the cuyahoga
gulls sail up the crooked air
to where the detroit-superior bridge leaps
and up across its arched spine
marches this black jesus
matted rasta hair and salvation army robes flowing,
horn in hand, dented apocalyptic bugle
blowing crazy
spastic notes flying sparse
rotgut wine inspired music
his melody line against
the blasting furnace below.

Robert Drake

Cleveland on Lake Erie

I watched her dress for a night out, a night about the city--
As she took off her garb of the daytime with an air of extreme intensity
Her temples were heavily pounding and her face was rosily flushed
Her movements were full of excitement as round and round she rushed
Her hair was a cascading softness against the gray mist of her robe
On her breast the sparkle of diamonds I saw as closer to me she strode.
She was regal and graceful and ample, but older I must insist
As she clasped the diamond bracelets about the great scars on her wrist.
Then she leaned over to look in her mirror, her glass right in the water
Fairer by night than by day, looking fairer by far than she ought to.
She was ready now for the evening, ready just for my sake
My beautiful, beautiful lady with her feet planted deep in the lake.

Mary Ann Lowry

The Heart's Cargo

Awake at last past Liberty's
Long snake of warning
Winged apocalypse
Gull scatter and wind
Our sulking wounds traffic
Toward the downtown spread
Sky rocks the eye
Does each white horse cry
Help me, I'm dying?
Light and the lungs shake loose
Vessels, feather and scale
Pitch to the elements
What crane can wrestle
With the heart's cargo?
Above the black-wreathed stadium
A cloud of sorrow, the Indians' sign
No home runs cheer Chief Wahoo
Only memory's running home grief
The face cracked open on the bridge
The tears flowing over the Cuyahoga
Come home, Daniel, your mother's dead
I fell in with the dreaming crowd
We worked the games a winning season
A hot dog lady, an orangeade kid
With no place like first place
No place like home
Still our harbor for dark desire
Now its victims wait
For my shoulder against the stone
Up the hill, trudge
To the halls of justice
In the distance gulls circle
Like buzzards over death

*Daniel**

13

When Rocky Colavito Played Outfield and the July Moon Was High

Have you seen the moon tonight,
higher than a pop fly?
Like a painted finger nail
or a wink of something gilded.
The drunken balloon man,
he has tried to buy the moon.

All the carnations are sold.
His wind-up walkie duckies
have marched back to brown bag farm.
Mickey Mouse, trapped inside a balloon
tied to a stick, has slipped through
the pocket holes of children in stadium shadows,

Who roam in urchin snips after dark
throwing major league pennants
over the bridge at the moon in the river.
They have swum in the inky, oily sky before
and freed the light in the street bulbs
with construction bricks,
so; once home in hollow rooms
they silently take a beating for everyone,
for us all.

From the window of the iron-railed
condemned escape,
the children see the moon tonight,
and dream the dreams of the outfielder,
Who, locked in the empty stadium
Where one game has ended and there are none until tomorrow,
stands this side of the fence
lapped in green paint grass,
his glove shining like magic
in the July night,
in the land where balloon men lay
with sleeping walkie duckies
who chatter no more,

All, just beyond the only escape
where the moon clears the broken street light
like some big leaguer,
by half a smile.

Tim Joyce

The Other Side of Love

JOE VOSMIK - - - - - - Cleveland Indians - - - - - - Critically Ill

"He was
        the sweetest swinger ever stepped in the box"
and now he was dying   cancer old fox
                had torn one lung to shreds
and the other was ripped by pneumonia
                it seemed like the lights
of his midnight hour were going to sleep

But I, I
        can remember a time when it was different
        a time when your father whispered
                                into your ear
        "That's Joe Vosmik"
        as if he were some kind of God
                a man's God perhaps
        but even Gods have their Achilles heel
and now Joe was having his.

As I
        trudged back thru the night to the dorm
        I thought about the moon
        about its other side
        and wondered why I
                        was suddenly
        glad for old Joe
                suddenly
        wishing for his death.

                                Doc Zbornik

Public Square

With camera, film and lenses
I sit and wait for city life with Tom L.
and his well-bundled friends.
Woolens in July? Never mind,
they are old and street wise and keep the faith
long after it is abandoned by those who can.

"NO, NO, NO, I'm not Pigeon Mary," she yells,
amid a flurry of feathers and a cloud of bread crumbs
scooped from ancient creased shopping bags.
The day old wonders sail from her knowing fingers
to impatient beaks.
Three bagsful and still they flock.

"No, Pigeon Mary, she's the famous one,
the one in the newspapers,
the one whose house they're trying to steal.
Me, I'm Pigeon Annie...
but you know somethin' -
I don't even like pigeons,
they're so fat and greedy...
Look over there,
those poor sparrows can hardly get somethin' to eat."

Behind me shuffles Fast Eddie.
His odor precedes his arrival.
Fast Eddie, agent to the birds and bums,
puzzled by my interest in pee-stained winos
and unkempt birds.

"Hey, you from Welfare? Police? F.B.I.?
Hey, you old enough to remember streetcars?
I'm the agent for these pigeons...
it'll cost you $500 for the rights to photograph them.
Hey, do you believe in pre-natal influence?
Hell, I don't.
When my mother was pregnant with me,
once she got mad and went around the house
breaking all the phonograph records.
and it didn't affect me, didn't affect me,
didn't affect me, didn't affect me..."

He snickers and shuffles.
He must hurry.
The mission closes at eight.

Barry Zuckor   17

William Hart

Don't look for Peaches
In the inner reaches of the city
Sitting pretty or shaking his hips
The way he once did on the strip
He's gone for good
Only his shadow dances
Where the street poor
Take their chances
Amid the breadcrumbs and the blood
That day the pigeons lost Hart
Their friend, and cried
The Monarch butterfly
I'd found on the sidewalk died
And I wondered whether
Their souls winged heavenward together

Daniel

steel & sadness

industrial tremors
            -earthquake of machinery
are bolted to dreams
and riveted to the sunrise.
rhyming smokestacks
the names of which
I cannot remember;
only their dark creases
oiling the black sun
with
brawn and muscle
        swinging hammers
of steel
        and sadness.
bloody work
        pouring into this
        cuyahoga.
endless sweat of tormented
Hungarian immigrants.
grimacing dogs chase them
to work in the Ruhr Valley
of Budweiser and Chevies.
towering girders
            of darkness
stand in the omniscient shadow
            of the terminal tower
giants of iron and steel;
the machine gun of the flats
form an assembly line of cream-faced boys
turned into tough bearded men
(on industrial terrain--
            its soft light sunsets
            its hard light moonshine)
nowhere to go
but round and round
in the late memory
of Daddy Maras
stopping off at Ellis Island
to get his name changed, shoes unshined,
hair uncut, religion changed
to that of J.P. Morgan.
coming to Cleveland, Ohio--
somewhere in the Middle Kingdom
of the streets are paved with gold
america,

vomiting his first night
on Franklin Ave.
drunk in america
at an Irish bar
(broken glass already
         --green and blue--
         shattered)
Daddy Maras
started a generation of coal smokers,
coke puffers, iron laughers, moon cringers,
blackly
taking the first job
in the first column
of the first want ad
they ever read.
         (shattered dreams
         --blue and green--
         on brick streets.)
stirring up iron and steel trouble
in the rollicking, rampaging union halls
of the 30's,
laughing and joking all the way home
in strike-torn Cleveland, Ohio.
sad eyed sons of Eugene Debs
calling for
industrial equality
on this
pitiful river
strung with gorgeous steel diamonds
and
belching with volcanic smokestacks of hate.
U.S. Steel quoth,
         "never more."
Jones and Laughlin,
         "never more."
Republic Steel,
         "we're the matador."

"you are the bullfight we've savored"
         we state
licking our lips in order
to swallow this red garment
of low wages
and dangerous work.

we're the time bomb of history
us tires
and spokes and cylinders and pistons
exploding on the horizon of night
    (beyond the faded memories of
    pastoral Hungarian streets)
we are the real fast paced
street car, Ford Motor, outa work
lock out
      (picking up the pieces
        of shattered glass and broken dreams.)
new job
7 am time clock
8 hour day immigrants
won another battle against steel barons
cops/cyclops with one eye in their foreheads;
the other eye blinded to the
bill of rights,
beating lawnorder
into some goddamncommieunion
who prays to the holy virgin on Buckeye Rd.
to not have sinned
in the deep Hungarian night
where the crucifix is tattooed
over the dollar sign.
paprika mixes with whiskey
smoldering red kisses
of immigrant boys
and fresh legged girls flushed
with lipstick;
Buckeye Rd. turns out another generation
of Saturday night shootouts
in the barrooms/bedrooms
of Hunky Town.
(sun poking through the eternal haze
of grey baked lake erie--
              shining on broken glass
              shattered and green)
aching memories that
Daddy Maras
is now dead.
fathers of steel are all forgotten
so sons can escape
this gut wrenching flood.

Daddy Maras
will not be mentioned again
until we return to
Buckeye Rd. for paprikash
and say a prayer on our
checkered tablecloth
       for a quiet
         moment
      of peace
for our embattled grandfathers
who clutched steel
in their ruddy hands
and tried not to cry
in front
of the bolted dreams
of what might have been
shattered like glass
on that trembling river
of steel
      and sadness.

Bill Arthrell

How to Be Like the Industrial North

Decorate yourself with the abandon of the city
a newspaper crumpled under each arm,
creased with sweat. Fill your pockets
with partial cigarettes and half
thought cigars. Keep the pigeon stable
on the crown of your head, make your eyes red
with the haze of fear and cushion
your feet
      with a mixture of small stones
          fine dust
      and splinters of glass.
Cover the ankles with labels of cheap chemical
wines that think grapes are legends.
Apply for federal aid.
Keep a knife handy to protect the wages
of misfortune and wear a sign advertising the site
of a famous battle or ghetto or default.
Watch yourself return to dust.

John Stickney

pints of cheap wine

broken blankets

glitter
in the alley

people
cut through
all day
this way, that way

from the gravel lot in your eyes
to the street in the mirror
where each winter
a few of them huddle
the wind blows thru
they pass around
a cigarette

two years before
working three-eleven
in and out all night
from the blast furnace
to a blizzard at five below
on the cuyahoga
that passes before sunup

Dennis McDonnell

Metal Sorter

I found you in the rusty air
of eastside steelyards
among heaps of stainless steel,
aluminum and die-cast.
I scraped your tarnished face
on the grinding wheel
to uncover your true metallic glint.
I looked for your spark or lack of spark,
touched you to polarized steel
to see if your core was magnetic or not.
I tried to verify your true nature.
Dabbing you with nitric acid
I waited for your reaction.
Do you turn green, brown, black or white;
or do you remain colorless and unaffected?
Are you copper, bronze, manganese,
red or yellow brass?
I came by you in my own way,
slogging along CTS bus routes
in winter dawns of pathetic sunrises,
among the noxious smoke
of burning lead, steel, plastic and diesel.
I groped through grease and filth.
snow and mud for your smallest particle.
I scrutinized you with the instruments of man.
Are you zinc, titanium, zirconium, monel,
nickel-silver, babbit or alloy?
I came by you in my own way.
You were the reason I struggled for the union,
the reason I despised management.
You were the bread on my table
the word in my mouth,
the anger in my chest,
the trash in my lungs.
You were the object of all my desires.

Peter Kastmiler

Ploughed Under

Of the homes that have been plundered--
High-gabled mansions of the past;
Have the wreckers ever wondered
Of the void the shadows cast?

Last night I caught the rose that swung
Across the porchway, sweet and red;
Waving in the summer breeze,
Just above my head.

And now the wreckers are here;
And now their iron ball has swung
In a dreadful arc, clean and sheer,
So coldly split, the rafters rung!

Beneath the roof a nest lies bare.
My sparrow tenants had fled in fear;
In rude protest they made me spare
Their grief I alone could bear.

Ben B. Berkey

Ode To A Bed

The man and woman who stretched upon this frame
and dreamt and woke and loved in it before us
are a long time dead.
                              Their journey was tremendous,
they had come from far away
            perhaps from Poland or Budapest

"You'll have full lives and beget many children in this bed."

The old fellow stank of basement juice
plum wine stained the yellow teeth
and with this gypsy wish
he passed his hands over us.

Outside in autumnal rain
you could smell the delicious steam
tumbling out from the Hot Dog Inn on forty-first and Lorain;

puddles, the gutters were matted
with a mush of piebald and orange leaves--
the approach of darkness quenched our bargain.

The walnut wood of our bed
is curved at the foot like a boat's bow,
the headboard swirls in a chipped fleur-de-lis-
the slats hand-sawed from fence posts,
four tiny wheels on the bottom of four legs;

we sail here we storm.
Once, in Ohio, in a tornado watch
without fear, here we made love.
There is no danger, no lightning bolt to blind us,
no room that is not our own
once we fall upon this wooden barge of dreams
floating, wandering.

                                        Tim Joyce

Growing Up Jewish in Cleveland, Ohio

It's difficult to sort out,
     square peg, round hole and such.
First, there were the crosses,
     my mother counting beads,
     father's raffle tickets
     and sister's uniform.
Men with florid faces blessed the
     house while sipping wine in
     white tight collars.
The murmurs of the good nuns
     filled the school.
Then, after four beers,
     the men slipped into brogues
     down at Tommy's
And their women peeked through
    · lace covered windows
     into the dark
     green
     streets.

John J. Stickney

Snow Sketch

Snow
flake down
the thinly veil
crusted white to walk on
like the River Jordan light-
testing my powers.
Snow
irk down
unscheduled,
unplanning the city's gold.

So whitely treacherous
yet fleecy downed
where dreams mesh the alabaster heaven
close to me
at the line grey
thin-stretched to lake, endlessly.

S. B.

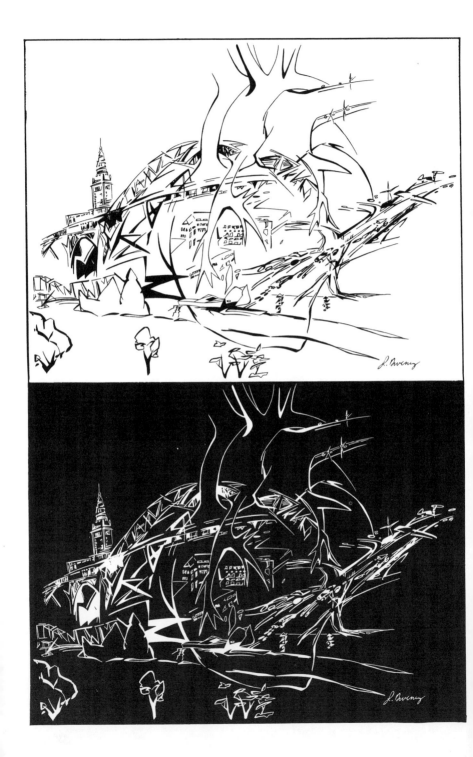

heartbreak

there's a heartbreak
    in the city tonight.
it rushes down
    avenues and boulevards
veins and arteries
    turning down city streets
around corners, crashing
    stop lights.
it pulsates, moves
    in traffic.
it's a bus, a taxi, a plymouth.
    it flows in its rivers
and empties in its lake.
    it spins in silver balls
on disco floors.
    it is drunk at corner bars.
it bleeds on hospital floors
    and is the voice of the
police siren in the ghetto.

this heartbreak
    is the ambulance quivering,
grimacing, tearing up the night
    with its terrible warning.
it is reflected in thundering
    skyscrapers
darkly waiting for the enormous
    night.
it is the bell that rings
    in the red school yard,
the grey phone that is not
    answered.
it is the tears
    in the mailbox and the cry
of the factory hawk at night.

it is drunk from every drink
    smoked in every cigarette
and dances with every dancer.
    it is laughed at by those with
no courage.

it is reflected/juxtaposed to the
stars and liquid planets
    of the night.
it is yellow from moonlight
    and the sap of trees from which
it tries to run.
    it is sad and strong and weak
and not the marriage
    of your wildest blue dreams.
it is the wedding in the slovak hall
    and the pierogies and vodka
devoured
    by those who wish
they were not.

it is this moment;
    not the last.
it is this city;
    not the next.
it cannot be sped past,
or willed to the future,
or nurtured into a garden of grey violets.
it is not my heart that
    is broken.
it is yours
    and it is I
    who have broken it.

Bill Arthrell

Hopkins/71 North

Out of futuristic, nightmare Hopkins
71 North . . . an arcade game
Passing cars that will never know second gear
& wondering what lane is under repair

Out the window, the glow
Of buildings of business
The terminal tower, a sentinel
A symbol, a signpost, minutes from my home

Freeway chess as the lake appears
Blackblue and slightly foaming
Liberty Blvd. to the right
The fast cool curves to the Heights

Marlene Lapars

Holy Week Sonnet, 1970

They blew off the Rodin statue's balls
Today in Cleveland. The picture on the news
Showed the Thinker flat on his back, his knees
Drawn up to shield those bronze genitals.
How can we describe what most appalls,
Anticipate the next attack? Our muse
Is an incessant harpy and like Yeats sees
The center cannot hold and everything falls.
But one good thing about that blast it got
The Thinker off his constipated can.
And Easter is the time for our conviction
To move us, to rake away the winter rot.
Did Jesus' mother say at the Crucifixion
It was for his own good, to make him a Man?

Donald M. Hassler

On My Haunches

Well, here I am
The kid who caught
For Local 2265
A million summers ago
On my haunches
Late afternoon
Behind the art museum
Green and quiet
With my dogs
The birds, the breeze
The good life, you know
Joggers jogging
Bicyclists biking
My dogs chasing them
Or each other or shitting
The big one, Josh, running over
Barking, scaring some poor guy
Away from a tree
Then pissing on it
Usually we're here under the stars
Around three A.M.: just us, the patrol cars
And my ragman roll of cold-eyed musings
Like when I turned forty, my waist was forty
When I was forty-one, my waist was forty-one
My age and my waist are keeping pace
So when I'm sixty-nine since I'm five, nine
I'll be sixty-nine all ways
Of course I won't be able to perform sixty-nine
Or any interesting number for that matter
One thing I'll be able to do, though
Is throw away my Sohio credit card
I won't need gas; I'll just roll to where I wanna go
Maybe I'll train my dogs to push me along with their noses
It might even become and Olympic event. But right now
Having just read in Rolling Stone that women dig ugly men
I'm still ugly enough to sleep with

Daniel[*]

p.s. to d.a. levy

The river doesn't burn as easily now
The collars have turned from blue to white
You don't even have to lie to women anymore

When my students ask me:
What were the 60's really like?
I give them your poems

When they ask me where you are...
I point to the sky

Barry Zuckor

The Speed of Night

the velocity of the moon
sears thru the open
city.

the speed of night
lights bars and avenues.

hurried stars sprinkle
the hopes of prostitutes
waiting in the long, slender
darkness.

the quickness of the subway
the rapidity of locking doors
the fastness of knives
the tip on the bar
the flicking of cigarettes.

the swiftness of police
sprints past
chrome and metallic.

stop signs, left turn, yield
all fester in the open wound
of night.

it happens so fast that
the sun has sunk
in that great lake.

quicksilver, mercury and
the speed of headlights
chasing something black
above the reflectors
on the shoreway.

Bill Arthrell

Lakeview Cemetery

That summer it was a short-cut home--
such a treat after work, the trees,
their cool green and oxygen. Bird voices clattering
as I'd move between the grey stone markers.

One evening, pushing through the hedges, fell onto
a garden! Tomatoes, peppers, squash--
tucked away among the tombstones
in the thick, fertile soil.

I took a tomato, round and perfect,
the size of my fist, and sat at the top of the hill,
the juice running red down my face
watching the sun set, and the lake grow dim.

Robert Drake

Midsummers Night Dog's Poem

for Daniel Thompson

At sunset we note
the Coventry crazy walker
recircle the park,
a June 22nd so hot,
like dog days a month early.

Our two dogs run and duck
while we, dog-tired, play watch dogs,
smile, forget ourselves:
we've gone to the dogs,
and they'll let us lie.

"Why Emma?" you ask.
"Means 'healer,'" I say.
"Like on a leash?"
"No, like in a wound."
"Maybe she'll do both."

The sun bleeds to its place
on this longest day.
From now on, shorter, darker.
And the real heat.
I follow Emma home.

Diane Kendig

Coventry

        slinks
forward,
        with the
action of a person
about to be sick,

leaning against
1926 bricks,
looking at
dirty
snow

Michael Drexler

The PCB Sparrow
for Kim Hill

Keeping my vigilance eternal
For the catcher of outlaw dogs
I let Truffaut run free in d.a. levy park
As I plumb the depths of the morning paper
Having come to the edge of Arabican ambience
To join the few, the proud
Those who wait out the decaffeinated coffee drought
Suddenly a sparrow tweets a greeting
Hey, Street Poet, how's Truffaut?
Do I know you? I ask as he lands on the comics
According to the latest pole he continues
I mean the one I just left across the road
From Coventry Books, in case of emergency or spill
When those PCBs are set free from their Pandora's box
You're to call the Coast Guard. CEI imagines you Coventry folk
Are so high, you can read the warning at bird's-eye level
The only reason I'd call the Coast Guard, I tell him
Would be to find out whether the coast is clear
You make sure your head is clear, he snaps
And mind your own PCB's wax. Here's the facts:
We are boxed in from sea to shining sea
I sing the box electric. Thirty-five million of them
Each offering our salad days a dressing of oil and toxic PCBs
You won't hear them ticking but they're time bombs
A hundred in this area explode every year
If only they all had silicone which is safe
But you know how slowly the corporations move
When it's costing them money. Let me put it this way
Cancer, cardiovascular disease, liver damage, abdominal pain
Skin lesion, reproductive failure, nervous disorder, respiratory...
Ok, OK, I say, I'll give the Coast Guard a call
I can just see the USS Cod coming up Coventry
Rescuing all the alkies who sit illegally on Irv's planters
Saving their livers from PCBs
And what of the lovely Dylan Thomas poets
You who have adventures in the skin trade
Reading in public, Bird adds
It's all right to be fat and read
But with bad skin from PCBs
Forget it. You'd better only publish

O phone pole ringed
With poisonous fruit, I emote
What a joke you play on us
You spill. You stay. You grow. You leak
There's a mad dog loosed in Eden
And nowhere to flee
O AT&T, O PCB, O CEI, O CIA
O spare us, says Sparrow and flies away
Looking for a clean, organic tree
As Truffaut runs by, barking goodbye
Headed for the same tree

                                    *
                          Daniel

Euclid Heights Blvd. Flows

Euclid Heights Blvd. flows......
      from humble beginnings
      she meanders at her leisure,
      languid and listless.
      past late model cars,
      dogs with people on leashes
      and discreetly hidden speed traps.
Euclid Heights Blvd. flows......
      beyond apartment houses filled
      with the upwardly mobile,
      beyond bonafide mansions
      hidden within tiny forests,
      separated from the world
      by moats infested with alligators.
Euclid Heights Blvd. flows......
      mingling with her tributaries,
      Fairmount above,
      Cedar below,
      like white water rapids
      headlong into Carnegie at rush hour.
      sharks, barracuda, and piranha
      descending to seek their level
      in the valley below.
      onward to commerce and business;
      into the land of giant shoeboxes
      standing on end....
Euclid Heights Blvd. flows......
      across the bridge into
      the west town shore
Euclid Heights Blvd. flows......
      again at evening tide;
      reverses her flow
      brings the fish home
      bare to the bones,
      empties them into
      the foothills of
      Coventry and Shaker
      and beyond....

John Bassette

Memoriam, Jesse Owens

We are all,
somehow,
lesser for it.
The slow run
moving
from the blistering pace...
    till world
was record; its
        fastest
            human.

Singly--
if but by seconds
(quaternary time)--he slowed
the mad rush
of an idea
in which he, and
life, had no place. He
symbolized the race. The
one he, part of, could
no more leave
than could others, to
date, wish destruction; even
the balest renegade of
every umber would grant
him that: he sped before
the eye of their death
and gained some reprieve,
some fashion of second start
for the race now
no more confined
to a cinder sprint
in a corner
of Berlin--but the
thoroughfare
connecting Delhi
and Moscow and Peking
and Buenos Aires; cities of the Americas;
Hamburg.

                    (Pheidippides,
"by birth an Athenian,
and by profession and practice
a trained runner," almost
without knowing
pleads: "Men of Sparta, the
Athenians beseech you
to hasten to their aid,
and not allow that state,
which is the most ancient
in all Greece, to be enslaved
by the barbarians.")
                                        His
going now stills
his speaking; living,
we knew his face: history
could (and thus we less
alone) have a human
one...

We leave,
that is, unable
still from Marathon
to hear him out: "Rejoice,
we conquer!" in no
small part,
with him.

                          James A. Miller

Saturday Night

   I wanted to call
a woman
   tonight for a date.

then I
was moonstruck
by a starry eyed
vision/ of glorious girls
/ strutting down Euclid Avenue/
with wine desire eyes/ luminous lips
/ gorgeous tasting star polished smiles/
red decked out in bright bosom dresses/ delicious
kissed evening smoldering with moon legged nylons/
high heeled lust dishing out Saturday night ecstasy.

   So, I never called my date.
   And Euclid Avenue,
   of course,
   was empty.

Bill Arthrell

Witness

listen he put that house on fire
same as he held a match to it

i see him sneakin in an outa there
wid a camera the other day

i bet he was takin pictures
of his ol lady and that other dude

you know   catchin em in bed and shit

he jist crazy enough to put em on fire

you know   last week
i be wipin down the car
and i see him kick the basement winda in

he see me too but he too pissed to care
bout makin a scene

i see him kick the winda in
then he cut his hand tryin to loosen it up
he cut it up bad   man

i see the blood all the way over here
an his ol lady start in on im for comin in
like that and bleedin all on the floor

he say   shut up   and start kickin her ass
right away   screamin bout her bangin the dude

she run out the house in her bathrobe
and take off in the car

he try to get her but she   lock   the   door
good thing

he stand there cussin an bleedin

i know he burn that house

nancy spider camposo

All Night

All night the streets are mine
Bits and pieces of shattered light
And far off against the caverned sky
Stalagmites of the burning city
But I am one to wander close to home
Find a path that twists between the trees
To a silver dollar near a bank
And catch the stream in its flux and ease
Did I say dollar?
More often it's merely change
Any way I get my money's worth
Motherless now
I feel I need
A deep connection with the earth
And all the night forces that call and beckon
In this dark kingdom of lovers and thieves
Sanctuary for a man of words
O look
The pocket where I hid my heart's been picked

Daniel

in memoriam, the sunbelt

peel away
            the terminal tower
                and arcade.
tear down the rows of
                        industrial
                        america
smokestacking the flats.
unpaint the italianate marvels
                of ohio city.
unpave euclid and superior.
uncomic
        (strip away)
            superman and bleed
            pink from
                ziggy's cherubic
                nose/life.
unrock the buzzard
            unSzellous the orchestra
and make stress sing reds
and greens (no blues
                fer you).
unethnic st. clair
unblack quincy
make jesse give back his medals
and rocky tear down the home run
fence.
make cleveland uneat its pierogies
ribs, paprikash, corned beef.
send hungarians and stadium
mustard back where they came
                        from.
unshine the sun
downtown the suburbs.
dispel the waters of
                erie and
                cuyahoga
and fell the woody
                    magnificence
                    of fairmount blvd.

unwinter
>　white steel waves
>　skiing
>　thru metroparks.
unspring lou at shortstop
robert on the mound
and joe as rookie of the year.
>　unblossom the summer
>　unfireworks it, too.
uncardiac the fall (and unorange
>　　　　　its leaves).
undrink a six-pack of beer
(and a quart of jamison's)
on st. paddy's day/old river rd.

unCleveland me
>　and I shall be
>　bought and sold
>　with the lawn furniture
>　and lack of autumn days
>　of phoenix and dallas.

Bill Arthrell

Red Cleveland

The color red along the highway
The steadiness of taillights, the passion
Of advertisers, red's ubiquity in signs
Tooth and nail, the bloody tracks of predators
Buildings ablaze, we are dazzled by this red-letter night
Is that a neon rose tattooing the brick?
Red flags of warning, red ball express
Incendiary cargo, the fugitive arsonist
His patriotic gas, the money in his pocket
Bursts into flame, the red ghost ranges
Over the lost wilderness, traffic stops in the name
Of lovely red...Chase Brass and Copper...Zagar
But O my favorite, this yellow darkening into red
Delicious sun the peach I eat

*Daniel**

Edgewater Park

Lakeshore colors mixed by forgotten
Beach to water the steel.

Footsteps of pride carry out
Mystical hours.

We are planted in each other's eyes
and the sun crosses us,
Yielding familiar dark light
Questions.

The city as spirit reflects
Each dimension
Like children
Asking sky.

Joel Garson